FENG SHUI

TODAY

WRITTEN BY TERRI REW

FENG SHUI

TODAY

WRITTEN BY TERRI REW

Dedication

"For Jeffrey and Katelyn who share
the magic of feng shui in my life."

Terri Rew

First published in 2000 by the Images Publishing Group Pty Ltd
and HBI, an imprint of HarperCollins Publishers
10 East 53rd Street
New York, NY 10022-5299

Distributed in the U.S. and Canada by
Watson-Guptill Publications
1515 Broadway
New York, NY 10036
Telephone: (800) 451 1741
            (732) 363 4511 in NJ, AK, HI
Facsimile: (732) 363 0338
ISBN 0-8230-6638-X

Distributed in Australia by
The Images Publishing Group Pty Ltd
ACN 059 734 431
6 Bastow Place, Mulgrave, Victoria 3170
Australia
Telephone: +(61 3) 9561 5544
Facsimile: +(61 3) 9561 4860
Email: books@images.com.au

Distributed throughout the rest of the world by
HarperCollins International
10 East 53rd Street
New York, NY 10022-5299
ISBN 0-688-17891-X

Feng Shui Today

Designed by The Graphic Image Studio Pty Ltd
Mulgrave, Victoria, Australia

Printed in Hong Kong

Contents

Introduction

*H*umans as visionary beings, continually strive for perfection in all they do. Having the ingenuity of producing an idea and following it through into reality is truly extraordinary. This is often reflected in the architectural design of buildings. Have you ever walked into a building and immediately felt peaceful, wanting to spend time browsing, admiring the shape of the building you entered and enjoying the color and interior design? If you have, then most likely you are experiencing the 'feng shui' of the building.

Feng shui (pronounced fung shway) literally means wind and water—both forms of important energy—one invisible, the other seen, yet most of life is dependent on them. Understanding the supremacy of these energies and their influence on the lives of people is the foundation of feng shui.

We all have intuitive responses and these feelings are evident when we buy a house or piece of furniture on its 'look and feel', without knowing why we buy it.

Feng shui is a science with mathematical formulas; but importantly, it is an intuitive science too. Over 3,000 years ago the Chinese realized that people were influenced in positive and negative ways by the layout, shape, design and orientation of their homes. After studying physical, seasonal and cyclic forces on land and in the heavens, the Chinese emperors used feng shui calculations to maximize positive energy in their palaces, surrounding buildings, and burial chambers. They believed that if surroundings changed, life changes would follow.

Scholars spent their lives studying the complicated ways of the world and universe so they could help improve the emperors' destiny. Over a period of time this sacred information eventually filtered down to the ordinary people, enabling them to live harmoniously with their environment without upsetting the laws of nature and karma too much.

Just as yoga enhances the lifeforce in people, feng shui enhances the lifeforce or *'chi'* in the earth. Chi flows through the earth like an underground stream, only varying its course when changes are made to the earth's surface by either man or nature, as in the construction of roads and buildings. In addition, the planet has its own energy lines that affect all life on the surface; even our homes and workplaces have their own chi.

Keeping this thought in mind, you can observe when a building is built, whether it will have a positive or negative effect on the environment. The actual shape of a building plays a vital part in feng shui. The ancient Chinese understood this and developed a system called 'The Five Elements'—wood, fire, earth, metal and water. The five elements system is ever present, residing over all life and can be described as energy tending to move in five directions. It radiates outwards, moves inwards, rises, descends and rotates, so to speak.

The five elements is a complicated energy system that relates to seasons, directions, body organs, food, color, shapes, planets, and much more. In this book we will focus on compass directions, shapes and colors in order to apply this knowledge to our own house or room immediately.

The shape and color of a building influences those working within such an environment. The element wood, as an example, is associated with the material wood, tall trees, cylindrical and rectangular shapes, and tall, narrow skyscraper buildings. The associated colors are green and light blue. Wood is connected with creation, nourishment and growth. Therefore, certain food establishments, nurseries and artists' studios benefit by working in a wood shaped building. In the home, the dining room is also influenced by the wood element.

On the other hand the element fire is associated with triangular shapes, sharp angles and points, particularly of roofs. Spires of churches fit into the fire element. The colors are shades of red and pink. Red is the color of blood so fire is associated with blood pressure and mental unease. Libraries, schools and other places of learning would go well in fire shaped buildings. In the home, the stove and open fireplace come under the fire element.

The element earth is associated with square, flat shapes, flat sides, flat roofs, and flat-topped low buildings. The material is brick, clay and concrete; colors are yellow, beige, tan, mustard, terracotta and cream. Earth-type buildings are solid and enduring. Storage space, seldom used rooms and garages would come under the earth influence for the home.

The metal element is associated with the round shape—domes, curved roofs, walls and arches, and the material metal; colors are white, gold and silver. Because the metal element is associated with finance, many banks and successful commercial premises favor a domed shape. This element is better suited to commercial and manufacturing businesses than to personal dwellings. Any commercial process involving metal, jewellery and hardware benefit from a metal building, and in the home, any area that is influenced by metal would be a great area for a workshop.

Finally, the water element is associated with undulations and irregularities of shape and construction, and the material glass. Colors are navy, black, and gray. The Sydney Opera House is a perfect example of a water-influenced building. Water is constantly changing, and so is linked to communication, media, word processing, literature, arts, advertising, and any commerce dealing in liquids (e.g. a dairy or brewery). In the house, the study could come under the water influence.

The five elements interrelate with each other and are cyclical. The 'Birthing' or 'Regenerating' cycle is:

- Wood gives birth to fire.
- Fire gives birth to earth.
- Earth gives birth to metal.
- Metal gives birth to water.
- Water gives birth to wood.

The preceding element also nurtures what it gives birth to—and so the cycle continues. The destructive cycle is:

- Wood digs up earth.
- Earth contains or muddies water.
- Water puts out fire.
- Fire melts metal.
- Metal chops down wood.

If you put this theory into buildings and place a metal shaped building next to a wood shaped building; the energy it creates will be inharmonious. More than likely the occupants in the wood shaped building will bicker with each other or suffer financial problems.

In this volume of *Feng Shui Today*, we will take a journey through beautifully designed buildings and rooms that have encompassed feng shui either knowingly or not and marvel at their design and shape, examining how the images present us with a feeling of serenity, success, expansion and a desire to spend time in them.

Feng Shui Today looks at combining the five elements into your living area only in a fun and simplistic manner. Readers who wish to take this concept further should consult any of the more in depth volumes available today.

I trust that reading *Feng Shui Today* will have a positive affect on your life and I wish your life to be enriched through the magic of feng shui.

Terri Rew

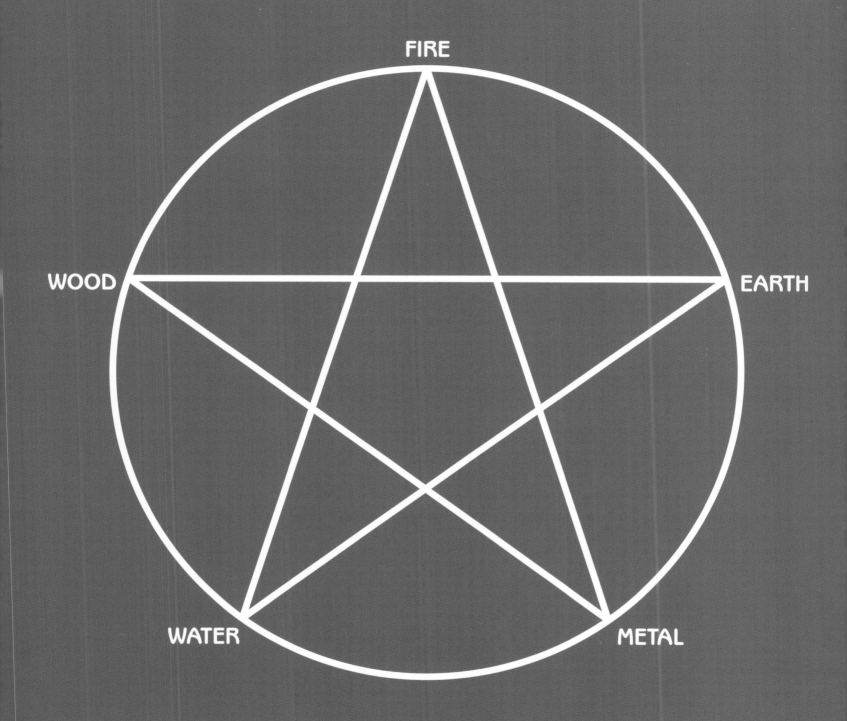

Chapter 1

Direction of your Home

Our home should nurture, heal and comfort us. This can be achieved if the correct feng shui forms and shapes surround the house.

Four requirements referrred to as Form School feng shui are necessary to enhance occupants' chi. They are called the Black Tortoise, the Green Dragon, the White Tiger, and the Red Bird.

The Black Tortoise (located behind the house), represents our foundation and stability and therefore it is considered good feng shui to have a solid backing behind the house. The Black Tortoise helps to hold and circulate life giving chi back to the occupants within the home, creating a sense of security and stability within the psyche. A Black Tortoise behind the house can consist of a high sturdy fence, tall trees, a double-story house or high-rise apartments—even distant mountains. Without this, chi may dissipate leaving occupants feeling depleted and nervy.

The Green Dragon sits on the left-hand side of the house looking to the front street. This is our activity side, so fast growing shrubs, plants, and trees are ideal on this side. Along with the garage and driveway; roadways, higher buildings and mountainous country are ideally located here. Sometimes when the Green Dragon is inactive, set-backs, procrastination and hassles can be experienced. Therefore always make sure the Green Dragon is activated. Lights positioned along this side may help.

The White Tiger sits to the right-hand side of the house looking to the front street. This is best suited for slow growing plants, vines, creepers, ferns, the vegetable garden and flowering shrubs in pots. This is our yin or inactivity area. When in balance, a sense of purpose may be experienced and if the Green Dragon is suitably activated, the energy flows to help create your desires. Many times I have heard my clients say that they experience delays or do not seem to be getting ahead in life when the White Tiger is stronger than the Green Dragon. Always strengthen the Green Dragon with activity if the White Tiger is too active.

The Red Bird represents what lies before the house. The area in front should be spacious and open if possible. Water views are considered auspicious for the occupants. In modern days, a roadway outside the front of the house is considered good feng shui.

If the front of the house is overgrown, dull, messy and hard to get into, chances are that life giving chi will not penetrate the house properly. This may result in occupants feeling lazy, sluggish, and messy.

The following pictures reveal natural and man-made form school feng shui.

Above: The rise of the hill behind the white house will create a Black Tortoise, while the front of the house is open and spacious creating a happy Red Bird to gather in chi.

Left: This house has a natural rising mound with trees behind it on top. This can act as a sufficiently purposeful Black Tortoise for the occupants, along with lots of open space in front for a reliable Red Bird and a low undulating hill on the right side for a White Tiger.

Below: The hills on the left-hand side of the house are higher therefore creating a well-placed Green Dragon.

Above: This picture shows Green Dragon mountains.

Right and opposite: The flat wide open stairway invites prosperous chi into this house. Form school is good as water sits in the front of the house. Careers may thrive for these occupants.

Right: The back of this house is supported by a natural mountain and creates a good foundation and stability for the occupants. The mountain will hold vital chi thereby enhancing career opportunities. A good Black Tortoise helps one create a stable work environment.

Below: A beautiful entrance with a perfect Red Bird in front of the house.

Opposite: An unusual example of good feng shui. The building on the right has a hill on its left reflecting a strong Green Dragon whilst the mountain behind is a great Black Tortoise. The building on the left is lower therefore creating a balanced White Tiger. The open space in front is a healthy Red Bird.

Top, left and right: These pictures show houses in which the occupants benefit from the high-rise behind them. The high-rise acts as a solid foundational support—a wonderful Black Tortoise.

Opposite: Sturdy evergreen trees behind this house help hold life giving chi and act as a barrier and foundation of a Black Tortoise for the occupants. The Red Bird in front has water that helps capture additional chi. Musical instruments are considered to have positive chi. The statue in the foreground is playing a flute, which is in itself uplifting at the best of times. This looks a peaceful and restful house to live in.

Above: The driveway to the right of the green house looking out to the street,
acts as an active Green Dragon.

Above: A meandering road outside the front of these town houses can be considered a good Red Bird. The medium flow of traffic passing may stimulate healthy chi flow for the occupants.

Above, below and opposite: An inner city example of 'hotel living occupants' experiencing a fabulously strong Black Tortoise behind them.

Chapter 2

House Shapes

House shapes can have an affect on our living environment.

A fundamental principle of feng shui is the dynamic 'five element' theory. According to feng shui doctrine, everything is made up of the five elements: fire, earth, metal, water, and wood. Understanding this cycle will give the feng shui consultant a deeper insight into harmonizing energies for his or her client.

When attempting to understand how the five elements work with each other, there are two main cycles to consider.

First there is the:

NURTURING CYCLE
- Fire enhances or nurtures earth.
- Earth nurtures metal.
- Metal nurtures water.
- Water nurtures wood.
- Wood enhances fire.

with the cycle forever repeated.

FIRE—EARTH—METAL—WATER—WOOD—FIRE etc.

This cycle creates balance and harmony and it's this harmony that a feng shui consultant will aim for.

Second, there is the:

CONTROLLING CYCLE
- Fire controls or melts metal.
- Metal chops or shapes wood.
- Wood digs up earth.
- Earth contains or muddies water.
- Water dampens or puts out fire.

FIRE—METAL—WOOD—EARTH—WATER—FIRE etc.

In this cycle, the energy is more dynamic and occasionally may be explosive!

Each element has several attributes associated with it. Throughout this book you will learn what these attributes are.

In this chapter entitled 'House Shapes', you will begin to understand how a particular shape and color is associated with each element.

Fire's unique characteristics are triangular and cone shaped together with sharp, piercing and pointed objects, and fire itself. Red, pink, purple, lilac, maroon, plum, and apricot are considered fire colors.

The earth element is associated with flat and square shapes, mountains and raised landscaping, and earth. Colors such as yellow, terracotta, tan, beige, mustard, brown, and cream are earth colors.

Metal has round, domed and curved shapes along with white, silver, and gold representing its characteristics. Anything made of metal, silver, and gold fit into the metal category.

The colors black, gray, and navy are water colors; and the shapes and objects are unusual, undulating, and wavy. Physical water plays a big part in the water element.

The wood element colors are all shades of green and light blues. Anything tall and rectangular in shape, and physically made of wood, is considered a wood element object.

Where there is balance in the nurturing cycle, in certain instances, the controlling cycle can be too harsh or strong to use. It is much better to use the nurturing cycle when designing a house.

木
WOOD HOUSES

This may be considered a wood element house, due to wood being used as a material. People living in a wood element house often boast an entertaining lifestyle; always on the go. The activity in this house may be one of sociability—lots of invitations to functions, lots of talk, laughter, and communication. It is a sociable energy—it's upward and rising, always expanding.

The water views from this house also enhance the wood element thereby creating lively, active conversation around the dinner table. If the occupants experience the downside of wood, which is irritability, shortness of temper, and inability to turn off, then lots of red, purple, maroon, pink, and apricot colors will help tone the energy down. Open fireplaces, electrical gadgets, red candles, oil burners, and any other red objects will do. These all fit into the fire element and as fire drains wood, it will create a feng shui balance for an over-active wood element house.

Opposite: A perfect place—feng shui says many happy and sociable dinner parties will grace this beautiful dining table due to the harmonic combination of wooden objects coupled with magnificent water views.

Above: Beautiful water views enhance the wood element, creating lively conversation.
Following two pages: The activity in this house may be one of sociability—lots of talk, laughter and communication.

Above: This is a wood element house in shape; it is tall, narrow and rectangular.

Opposite: This house can be considered a wood element house because it is literally made of wood; particularly take notice of the rectangular shaped chimney.

土 EARTH HOUSES

Left: This house is a great example of an earth element house. In this example it is more the boxed style and square windows that give the house its earth element appeal. Usually earth element houses promote nurturing and caring feng shui energy for occupants, although sometimes earth energy can drain occupants. The trick is to find a healthy balance.

Opposite: An excellent example of an earth house. It is square, boxy and beautiful—the windows are even earth shaped in appearance.

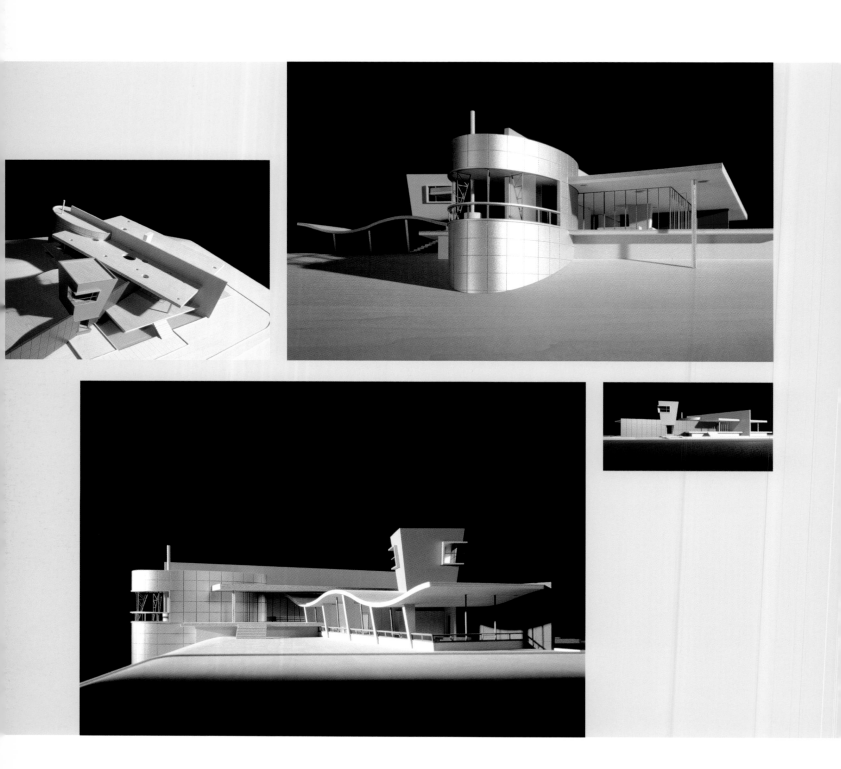

All pictures this page: A house that has plenty of curves, sharp angles, squares, and rectangles—perhaps the water element is best used to describe this enchantingly unusual house.

Above: This is indeed a true water element house that incorporates many colors, shapes, and angles. Water is associated with communication and ideas.

Right, below and opposite: The unusual shapes, curves, and the use of glass, give rise to the water element which promotes creativity and ideas, so one may feel inspired living in this house.

Above: The sharp pointed roof is considered a fire shape. Notice the window line ends in a pointed finish—it looks ready to take off and fly! Such is the energy of fire.

Opposite: The triangular shaped red brick fireplace, along with red and purple décor, create a wonderful fire element room. Interestingly, the yellow colors belong to the earth element—earth drains fire. This is part of the nurturing cycle, so conversation and gatherings around the cosy fire will be warm, intimate and friendly. A great place to spend time!

金
M E T A L   H O U S E S

Opposite and left: The pleasing curved lines this house has creates a wonderful metal element feel.

The Metal element is associated with wealth, but can also reflect intelligence and sharpness of mind for people living in a metal shaped home.

*M*ost residential houses will have certain shapes, colors and objects determining which of the five elements they belong to. More often than not, we have a combination of two or more different types. If possible, it is best to have a combination of all five to create equilibrium.

You could say that this beautiful house has the combination of all five elements—fire, earth, metal, water, and wood.

Outside it is square, boxy, and painted in earthy tones, with tall, rectangular windows and doorways. Inside it boasts a beautiful and good feng shui stairway. The graceful curve can fall into the metal or water element. The stairway is solid which means it gathers and lifts chi up to the next level. Gaps in stairways will leak the house's energy thus creating chi blocks.

Vibrant splashes of maroon, and reddish colors give the fire element the chance to produce some yang (activity) energy. The house looks inviting and one could imagine a good dinner party, with great conversation happening well into the early hours of the morning.

Opposite: The solid stairway gathers and lifts chi up to the next level.

Chapter 3

The Feng Shui Garden Color Ring

Feng shui is described by many as an art, a science, and a tool to enhance one's way of life. In reality, it is a powerful and dynamic energy force that may help our personal life reach greater heights.

The object of good feng shui is beauty and balance. If something looks beautiful it creates a sense of peace and a desire to spend time in its surrounds—this is the case with where we live. It is essential that our living environment pleases us to look at. If we walk through a delightful garden with delicately perfumed scents floating in the air, it creates a sense of serenity and delight. We then bring this energy into our house. On the other hand, if we walk through an overgrown, weed infested garden, it displeases our senses and looks ugly to our eye. We will bring this energy into our house, either consciously or unconsciously. Therefore, it is important to create a 'Feng Shui Color Ring' for your garden.

The feng shui color ring is planting and growing plants according to their color relationship with the direction in which they sit. The previous chapter mentioned each of the five elements and their many associations.

In addition to these associations, the five elements, fire, earth, metal, water, and wood also have an association with the eight compass directions of north, south, east, west, northeast, southeast, southwest, and northwest. In this, the

- Fire element is associated with south.

- Earth element is associated with northeast, southwest, and the center of your house.

- Metal element is associated with northwest and west.

- Water element is associated with north.

- Wood element is associated with southeast and east.

Summing up the association of the five elements, we see that the fire element likes sharp, pointed, and triangular shapes, together with the colors red, pink, purple, lilac, plum, maroon, mauve, and apricot. Objects include open fireplaces, candles and oil burners, barbeques, and any other fire-like objects. The fire element's associated direction is south.

The earth element likes low, flat, and square shapes and objects. Landscaping using earth is considered an earth element, along with sand and mud. Also, anything made from terracotta, clay, earthen ware, ceramics, concrete, and porcelain are considered earth objects. Its colors are yellow, terracotta, tan, beige, mustard, brown, and cream. Its associated directions are northeast, southwest, and the center of the house.

The metal element likes round and curved objects and shapes. Anything made of metal is naturally a metal object; a metal sculpture in the garden fits nicely into this category. Its colors are white, silver, and gold. The associated directions are northwest and west.

The water element likes wavy, undulating and unusual curves, shapes, and objects; ponds, water fountains, wishing wells, fish tanks, pools, and spas are water objects. Its colors are black, navy, and gray. The associated direction is north.

The wood element likes tall, rectangular shapes and anything made of wood, along with plants, trees, shrubs and flowers. Wood colors are all shades of green and light blue such as sky and powder blue. The associated directions are southeast and east.

From recognizing that each of the eight directions has a color association, you can plant shrubs, flowers, plants and trees around your garden according to the direction and its color.

Keep in mind the nurturing cycles (see p 26) when planting, as you can use a color from that cycle as well. It is best not to use a controlling element color when designing your garden.

For example, when planting in the west which is metal, the colors are white, silver, and gold. Earth nurtures metal so additional colors of yellow, mustard, tan, brown, beige, cream, and terracotta can be used. However, you can avoid colors like red, purple, pink, and apricot that are from the fire group as they are part of the controlling cycle. Fire controls metal.

Also keep in mind when an element nurtures the one after it, it becomes drained. For example, fire nurtures earth. Although earth is strengthened by fire, fire is, in itself, drained as it is giving all its energy to earth.

Above: These flowers belong to the fire element color group—shades of pink and red. They blend well together and create a harmonious feel to the garden.

 49

FENG SHUI COLOR WHEEL

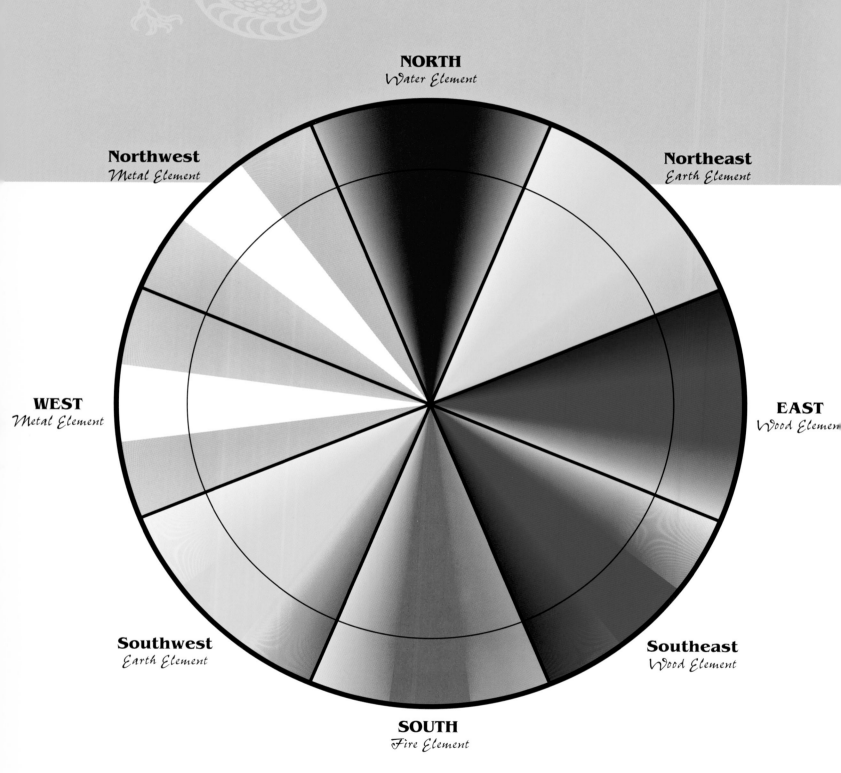

NORTH
Water Element

Northwest
Metal Element

Northeast
Earth Element

WEST
Metal Element

EAST
Wood Element

Southwest
Earth Element

Southeast
Wood Element

SOUTH
Fire Element

Familiarize yourself with the eight directions of your compass inside your house by using a compass in the center of the color wheel. Stand in the center of your house or nearby, and place the compass and the color wheel either on a table or on the floor, aligning the arrow with north.

Once you establish where north is, then familiarize yourself with the other directions around your house. Your house is divided into the eight compass directions. Some houses that are L-shaped or are unusually built have directions missing within their house. As a cure for this, you can plant the appropriate colors in your garden.

Now draw the eight directions on your house plan from the center of your house and extend it to the boundaries of your property.

Some people may be content to visualize approximately where their boundaries are and may not wish to draw it on a house plan. This is fine.

Now, let's plant our garden according to feng shui colors:

The north sector or direction can have colors of white, silver, gold, navy, black, and gray. Remember metal, (white, silver, and gold) supports water (navy, black, and gray.)

Northeast can have red, pink, purple, lilac, mauve, plum, maroon, yellow, terracotta, tan, mustard, beige, cream, and brown colors. Remember northeast is an earth element and fire (south), (red and pink), supports earth (yellow and cream.)

East and southeast colors are navy, black, gray, and all greens and blues. Water (black, gray, and navy) support (wood), greens and blues.

South has greens and blues along with red, pink, purple, maroon, plum, mauve, and apricot. Green and blue (wood), support (fire) red.

Southwest has red, pink, purple, maroon, plum, mauve, apricot, yellow, terracotta, tan, mustard, beige, cream, and brown (southwest is an earth element.) Fire (red) supports earth (yellow.)

West and northwest have yellow, terracotta, tan, mustard, beige, cream, brown, white, silver, and gold. Earth (yellow) supports metal (white.)

Please note that the above color scheme incorporates the element color and the preceding nurturing element color.

Chapter 4

Above: "...This renowned symbol is known as the Tai Chi. It is a mandala
for contemplation, and it reveals the meaning of life on many levels.
The circle represents the Ultimate Source, and within the circle the two
forces of yin and yang are represented. They can be described as two
magnetic poles—positive and negative—which are constantly
interacting and creating movement. Together they create life."

Extract from *The Feng Shui Garden* by Gill Hale, Publisher—Hodder & Stoughton.

Beautiful Rooms

Whether we believe in feng shui or not may depend on how we arrange our living space. For those who have an understanding of feng shui, clutter is abhorrent in every way and a beautiful looking living space will be essential to one's well-being. Clutter is the Number 1 enemy of feng shui. If you have clutter and mess, it depletes your energy.

Therefore our living spaces flow much better when they are clean, neat, and beautiful to look at. Having a beautiful room, and creating it with awareness, brings balance and harmony into your life. To do this action in the first place is to have an understanding of the principle of yin and yang.

Feng shui is all about maintaining the balance between yin and yang. Each has the embryonic seed of the other within it. If one force reaches its extreme, it changes into the other. It is this very concept of change that is at the heart of Chinese philosophy.

Yang energy can be expressed with daytime, sunlight, open spaces, heat, activity and movement, and so much more; whereas yin energy is night-time, moonlight, solid and cluttered areas, inactivity, and coldness along with a myriad of many other descriptions.

Bedrooms are yin spaces and should be in a quieter part of the house. The bedroom is a place of rest and recuperation and should not have any distractions such as a TV or radio blaring in there. Noisy motorways outside the front of the bedroom window is very yang and will disturb occupants' sleep patterns.

Lounge rooms and dining areas have much activity going on and are considered the yang areas of the house. Naturally TV, radios and general activity in these rooms will keep the yin/yang principle in balance.

The five elements will be present in a varying degree in most rooms. The following is a brief explanation of each energy and the feelings associated with them:

- The wood energy within a room symbolizes growth and expansion—it encourages socializing, laughter, fun and creativity.
- The fire energy in a house relates to much excitement, happiness and maybe a little full-on energy. Fire energy can encourage passionate debates and forceful energy in a room.
- Earth energy in a house denotes a caring, nurturing environment. It creates a sense of dependability. It is stable. One may be drawn to an earth room when feeling unwell or in need of solitude.
- Metal energy in a house can create a feeling of success and wealth. It has the feeling of gathering and accumulating; it draws you in. So metal rooms may attract occupants to discuss financial situations or invent ideas on how to make money.
- Water energy rooms can enhance communication and help one achieve knowledge. It helps one to contemplate life.

In the pictures which follow, you will view rooms that people have intuitively set up—some may already have been aware of feng shui. Regardless, the rooms have certain feng shui characteristics that create energy within their homes. Often rooms will have either a blend of each element or will be predominantly one element.

Certain pictures reveal rooms full of exciting feng shui shapes, colors, and objects—some may be yang in appearance, others will be yin. Either way, some if not all of the five elements will interact with each other.

This room has a predominant wood energy due to the wooden walls and floor. The large baseball picture represents activity and wood is an excitable energy. The two energies combined may create a room that is very yang. However, the red chair is a fire color also yang in nature—it drains wood and acts as a good feng shui balance for this room.

The striking use of the color red makes this a delightful fire element room. This is a typical yang space enhanced by yang element fire. The plants and terracotta tiles add wood and earth to create a good feng shui balance.

Above: A strong yang room that has wide, open spaces and allows plenty of light to enter. However, when people do not sit with their back to a solid wall they can become restless as the chi does not support them. The tree placed in the courtyard along with other shrubs helps capture and hold escaping chi.

Opposite and following four pages: Open-house plans can be very good feng shui. However, plants used in certain areas act as a natural barrier for escaping chi and hold it there. Plants placed under open slatted stairways push up vital chi to the next floor.

Above: The round cornice above and the circular table harmonizes *sha*
(negative) chi between two rooms.

Above: Good furniture placement allowing great chi flow, although it is best
not to have a chair with its back to an open door.

Above: The bold use of red for walls and ceiling make this a wonderful
example of a yang, fire energy room, supported by wood—a fabulous room
for inventing many creative ideas.

Above: This white woodwork acts as a perfect barrier for escaping chi at the
base of stairs directly facing a door.

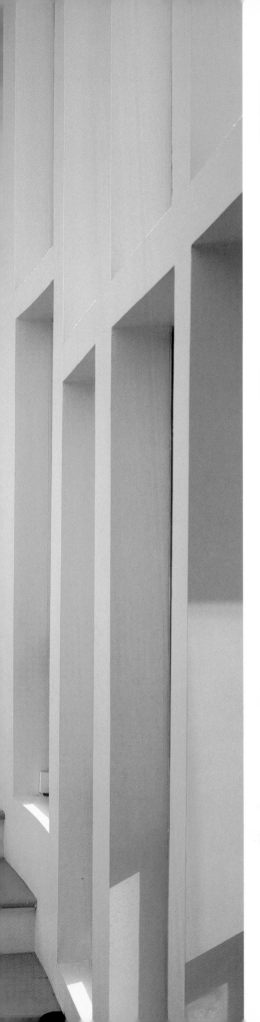

Opposite: A beautiful example of a metal element stairway; its graceful curve and serene pastel color create the metal element feel.

Above: White represents the metal element; metal energy creates a wealthy feeling.

Left: Plants in windows create an excellent chi barrier for escaping energy.

Far top and bottom: Totally wood element energy. If you like beams in your decor then make sure you don't sit or sleep under them as this may cause unease.

Opposite: In the background is a cone shaped tower which represents the fire element; the foreground has a wooden desk and inside there are wooden floorboards and wooden chairs. The wood energy supports the fire structure and therefore too much energy could be left unremedied.

The stone statue is an earth cure therefore creating a harmonious flow in the five element cycle. Wood nurtures fire which nurtures earth.

An excellent example of a stairway well placed. Important chi does not escape out through the front door.

Above: It is always good to have an object, picture or plant at the end of a long corridor to soften the energy and to create a good look.

Center and opposite: A gently flowing metal energy stairway. Graceful curves send chi upwards in a spiraling motion; the plants at the base help gather and send energy upwards as well.

Square and boxy shapes along with brick flooring and sandstone walls create an earth element feel. Tones of red are fire with yellows and ochre representing earth. A great place to be for nurturing and comfortable talks over dinner.

Above: The rectangular dining table is a wood shape, therefore great conversation may be generated during dinner parties. The metal element in the chair frames is control of wood (table shape). In the controlling cycle metal controls wood. This can create money, so profitable business dinners may result from this combination.

Below: This is an interesting interaction between wood (walls, floor and table), and metal with the round shape of the table, round dried flower arrangements on the walls, and the white couch. Earth is represented by the sandstone bench and square shaped windows. This is balanced by the water on the table and the fire colored flowers of red.

Above and below: A great feng shui kitchen as food can be prepared in the open while facing everyone. It is not good to have your back to an open door or window when preparing food; it can draw nervous chi into food.

Opposite and above: A good feng shui kitchen as the burners enable the
'cook' to face the room rather than have their back to the room. This creates
a settled subconscious mind whilst preparing food.

Above: The round metal plaque is a perfect metal element to place between the two bookshelves; it creates good visual balance. Although metal controls wood in the five element cycle; here it tends to control the closed-in feeling created by the shelves. Additionally, the spiked plant in the foreground has fire element shapes and sits upon a fire shaped stand (triangle with spear points) helping to control wood even more.

Top left: Another example of shelves either side without the balance of the metal plaque to soften them.

Bottom left: Anything with curves always creates a good chi flow.

Opposite: A long corridor can tunnel fast chi, so the piano at the end of this corridor helps soften fast chi flow. Interestingly, a piano or any musical instrument is considered good feng shui as it lifts up the energy in the room creating a peaceful feeling.

Above: If there is a large window at the base of your bed then hang heavy curtains across the window and close them at night—this will prevent vital energy being depleted from your body at rest.

Opposite: The V-shaped window is a fire element shape. It is tunneling fast fire energy towards the occupants' heads. Too yang—this could be enough to cause restless sleeps. The bedhead is made of metal and has a water element appeal due to the undulating and wavy shapes. Fire controls metal and water controls fire. The bedhead may be the perfect remedy for this interesting fire shaped window.

Left: A view to the world. Although a magnificent vista is beheld, too much chi can flow in, therefore a round table helps the energy flow more evenly.

Opposite and below: The colors are fire, the pillars and table are metal along with the curved design, and the construction is earth. A delightful balance of fire nurturing earth nurturing metal. One may enjoy lazy afternoons in this courtyard.

Top left and right: Whether the designers had an understanding of feng shui or not, they still created a good feng shui cure with the arched entry gate leading into this complex. The arch helps slow down fast chi flow and circulates energy evenly.

Bottom: A metal element feel with the color of white, round pillars and metal light fittings. Metal energy is associated with money and this verandah certainly has that feel.

Opposite: A real earth house, built entirely with a great variety of earth products.

Below, center, opposite and following two pages:
Imaginative splashes of colors, shapes,
ornaments and objects—the five elements
expressing themselves. This may be useful for
people needing creative inspiration. On the other
hand it may create too much activity for certain
individuals.

Opposite, top left and right, bottom left and right: Another bold style using labyrinthine quality with colors, shapes and more objects from the five element group. This house has the center as open plan and is considered good feng shui as energy circulates freely.

Following two pages: An open area in the center of the house is considered good feng shui—energy is able to circulate freely, thereby creating a sense of expansion, prosperity and creativity. Occupants in this house may feel inspired.

Opposite, above and below and following four pages: Another multi-element house using the colors. This place tends to lean towards an earth feel in so much as boxy shapes are predominant. Even the red bay window is earth shaped in appearance but painted a fire color. This house could well create nurturing from a hectic lifestyle while still inspiring creativity and work related ideas. Observe the stairway and doors entering the house. The flow of chi through two doors may create lots of activity for the occupants.

All pictures on pages 106 and 107: Well placed and pleasing objects in a room are beautiful to the eye. This in itself is good feng shui.

All pictures on pages 108, 109, 110 and 111: Another example of a beautiful looking house—the wooden arches (pictured opposite) symbolically represent a train track. This can be good feng shui as it helps move chi around this big open plan house.

Above: This house could well be considered an earth and fire element house due to it being made of sandstone, brick and concrete while nestled into the earth itself. Fire is represented by the sharp pointed roof. Earth energy denotes a nurturing and stable environment.

Left: Open living yang room with beautiful Red Bird vista. The fireplace central to the room, along with the magnificent view will enhance great conversation and a lively atmosphere.

Right, below left and right: These rooms look great, feel great and invite a richness of living. This in itself is good feng shui.

Left page: This enchanting house although made of wood, is also considered metal energy due to the roundness of design. Metal is often associated with wealth; metal controls wood which is wealth to metal.

Left and below: A good metal element feel; lots of white along with curves in stairway.

Above, left and opposite: The curved aches on the wall and the eight sided star (pictured left) help circulate chi to the upper floor of this two-story open plan house. Objects as shown, can always be used to help direct important chi throughout the house.

Right: It would be best to turn the table and rug the other way as vital chi can escape through the open doors this way.

117

Opposite, above left and right: Open living is liked by most people; however chi tends to flow out from windows that do not have blinds. Plants positioned by windows reduce chi flow, and create an attractive look and feel while allowing the view to remain unobscured.

All pictures on pages 120 and 121: Whether water is an element that agrees with you or not it does create a peaceful and serene outlook, and often is good to walk or sit near to contemplate life's changes and challenges.

If placed according to 'Flying Star' [see p 171] it will also enhance wealth and prosperity.

All pictures on pages 122, 123, 124, 125, 126 and 127: This house has a beautiful feel to it. It looks graceful, chi flows smoothly and the many fine pieces of furniture displayed create a warm and inviting place. The rounded columns, the light color scheme and round open appeal create a metal feel; metal denotes gathering and accumulation—a gathering of riches. An angel always acts as a protective measure when placed inside a house.

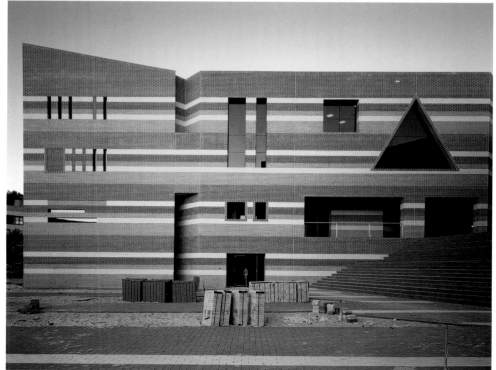

Opposite, top and bottom: This building is the New Technologies Building. It is interesting to note that it uses wood and fire shapes, balanced by earth in concrete and brick materials—so an elemental balance is occurring. Wood nurtures fire which in turn nurtures earth.

Wood denotes upward movement, expansion and creativity, while fire is energy at its fullest—it radiates outward and represents motivation and movement. Earth creates the stable environment to house this energy. This building may invent some very useful ideas and tools for our future generations.

Forms such as roadways, houses, trees, shrubs, mountains, and rivers have an influence on our environment. If something looks friendly and attractive then the energy will be affected. On the other hand, if the form nearby looks frightening or overwhelming, then the feeling around the house may take on its energy imprint. Always make sure that trees, shrubs, and other dwellings do not have a sinister appeal about them.

Above: A well placed stairway; it is graceful and curvy and draws chi up easily.

Above center and right: A very bright and lively room with many open windows—lots of yang chi. People may, however, feel too exposed in this room and tend to shy away from it. The solution is to hang curtains on the windows.

Opposite: Long, straight corridors create sha chi. The cross on the door along with colored glass can act as a natural chi barrier, therefore preventing important house energy from leaking out.

Top: The palms at the window act as a natural energy barrier because they are arched. This allows chi to circulate evenly rather than rushing out through the window.

Bottom: Pictures, lights, skylights, objects and ornaments along straight corridors soften the appearance and prevent energy from traveling too fast.

Above: A wonderful feng shui remedy for a slanted ceiling. The colorful streamers act as an inventive idea to draw chi upwards, away from the bedhead.

Above and opposite: Examples of fire shaped objects—the triangular table, red chair and pink cushion, and pink triangle border around the rug. Also representing fire shapes are the pink candles and black and brown triangles on the bench, red wall in the background, and red flowers.

Above: Good furniture placement. It is always best to corner lounge and chairs if possible. This helps to circulate chi evenly.

Top right: Two or more doorways together create sha chi. The energy flows too fast and straight—the round glass table and black chairs help disperse energy in a gentle way.

Bottom right: Feng shui says that if preparing food with the back to an open door or window this may lead to negative energy going into the food. The mirrored fridge door acts as a natural feng shui remedy as it enables one to see behind while preparing food.

Opposite: Another smart way to lift energy to the next floor is by the use of uplights. Light is good feng shui at the best of times; these curved uplights give this room an inviting and warm appeal while circulating healthy chi.

Above: The lattice placed in front of the entrance stairway acts as a good chi barrier by hindering vital energy flowing out through the stairway. The patterned mosaic will act as a positive upliftment for chi.

A mural or picture with depth can be used to visually balance a room
windows or doorways. Although this room does not carry this disadva
the mural in the background gives more depth and intrigue.

Opposite: Wood energy is very dominant in this room so lots of interesting and perhaps heated discussions may happen over dinner.

Bottom: The urn at the end of the corridor acts as a chi barrier thus preventing good chi from flowing out of the window from the corridor.

Top: Feng shui suggests it is best to have clear flowing lines and not have clutter as it stagnates chi. This kitchen is clear and spacious.

Right: Angels are always considered good feng shui for any place.

Opposite: Square shaped granite tiles create an earth element bathroom.

Above: Arches and rounded objects are always considered good feng shui—they help circulate chi.

Right: Natural water views at the front of the house are considered good feng shui, indicating a healthy Red Bird. The Red Bird represents the energy in front of your house and how it can enter. If open, clean, beautiful, and inviting then the occupants may experience good health and vitality.

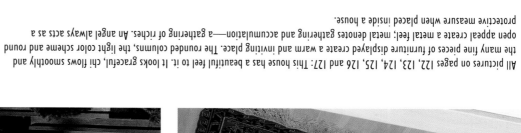

All pictures on pages 122, 123, 124, 125, 126 and 127: This house has a beautiful feel to it. It looks graceful, chi flows smoothly and the many fine pieces of furniture displayed create a warm and inviting place. The rounded columns, the light color scheme and round open appeal create a metal feel; metal denotes gathering and accumulation—a gathering of riches. An angel always acts as a protective measure when placed inside a house.

Chapter 5

Remedies, Solutions, and Trouble Shooting

Barrier between cars and houses

Light repels sha chi

Ground trellis acts as barrier if there isn't a fence to block house from cars

Cars

The aim of enhancing feng shui is always to encourage life giving chi to meander throughout the house to promote good feng shui and improve occupants' health. Chi is considered negative (sha) when traveling in a straight or fast way. This chapter is designed for problem areas and what follows are those questions most asked of me in my seminars and workshops.

T-INTERSECTION

Any house that sits on a T-intersection at the end of a long road, has sha chi attacking it. This is considered inauspicious and occupants may suffer with nervous complaints and/or money loss, irritability, and other vague complaints associated with their health.

Certain Masters have explained that the subconscious mind cannot discern between reality and non reality in relationship to feng shui energy.

For example, people who live on a T-intersection will see cars coming up the street towards their house, turning either left or right into the road in front of their house.

The subconscious views each car coming towards the house as a potential threat—careering out of control and colliding into their house.

The reason for this is because sha chi is traveling at a fast rate, hitting the house each time a car drives up the street— the subconscious is on the alert for danger all the time. Eventually this drains the occupants' energy.

REMEDY

Place a barrier in front of the oncoming traffic and the house. This is best achieved with a high fence or lots of trees and bushy shrubs in front.

Sometimes this proves to be impractical. The next best remedy is to place a ground trellis in front of the front door or front bedroom and lounge room windows. Hang flowering pots or grow vines on the trellis to make it look attractive. This will help shield the house from unlucky sha chi.

Another good remedy is to place a tall, round bulbed light at either side of the path or driveway, and switch them on for a few hours daily. This helps repel sha chi. Never put a convex mirror on the front fence facing the oncoming traffic. The energy can be too strong and cause an accident, or it can draw the sha energy directly into the house.

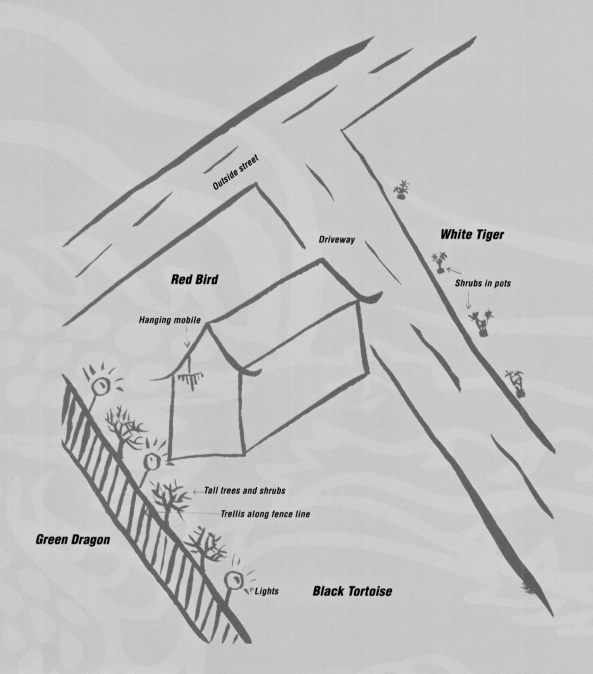

Outside street

Driveway

White Tiger

Red Bird

Shrubs in pots

Hanging mobile

← Tall trees and shrubs

── Trellis along fence line

Green Dragon

Lights

Black Tortoise

MY DRIVEWAY IS ON THE WHITE TIGER SIDE

Imagine standing at the front of your property with a road in front of you, looking at the house on the opposite side of the road. The left-hand side of your house is the Green Dragon; the right-hand side is the White Tiger; to the back is the Black Tortoise; and in front is your Red Bird.

A driveway is best located on the Green Dragon side as this side is your yang or active side and a driveway stimulates active energy. Often the driveway is on the White Tiger side.

REMEDY

Always strengthen the Green Dragon side. You can do this by installing two or three lights along the fence line; maybe even consider solar lights. The Green Dragon is your active side and requires activity and movement. If there is a door, use it. Even a clothes line on the Dragon side will add activity here. Additionally hang a mobile (not metal wind chimes) but a twirling, wooden one, in the colors of red and green. Plant fast growing trees or put up a trellis along the fence line. The idea is to create movement and height.

To soften the White Tiger side, put flowering shrubs in pots and position along the White Tiger side.

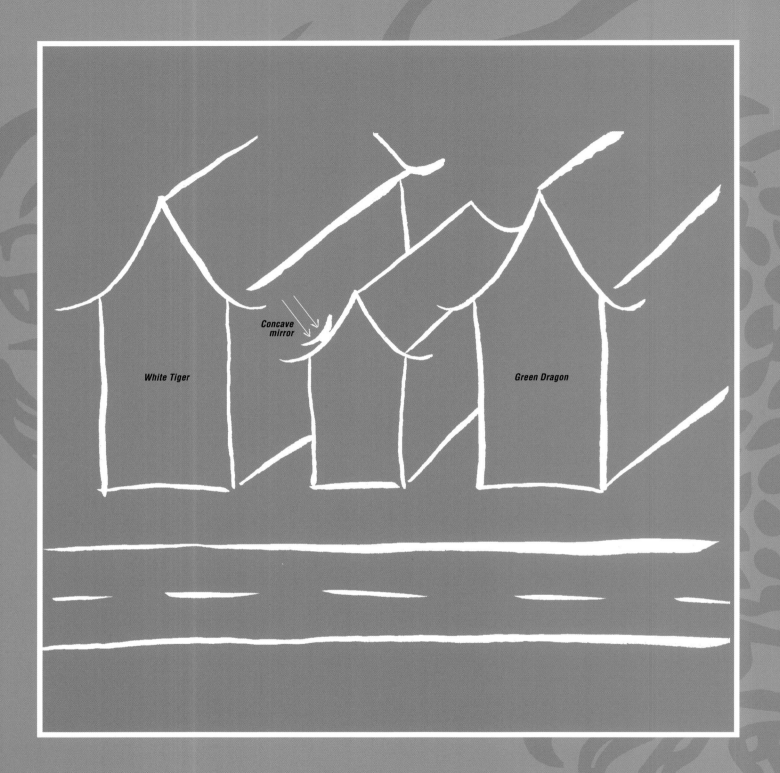

White Tiger

Concave
mirror

Green Dragon

TALL POPPY SYNDROME

If your house is surrounded by two-story houses or
large blocks of flats, put a concave mirror on top of
your roof on the White Tiger side and aim it at the
house next door. The concave mirror draws vital chi to
your house and helps soften the White Tiger's energy.

POISON ARROW

Any sharp point in the form of neighbor's eves and gutters, sharp angles on buildings or anything that is sharp and pointed facing your house, may be considered a poison arrow.

A poison arrow gives off sha chi (harmful energy) and may cause concern to whoever it reaches. For example, if your neighbor's house has a sharp roof or gutter pointing towards your front door, bedroom, or office, chances are the sha chi may be affecting you. Sha chi affects you when unexplained things go wrong in the house—you experience pockets of bad luck for no apparent reason, or feel irritated and drained. Maybe plans go astray, or relationships with neighbors are strained. If unexplained obstacles are occurring and you discover you do have a poison arrow situation, then apply the following remedies.

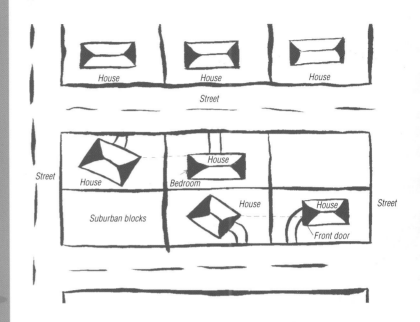

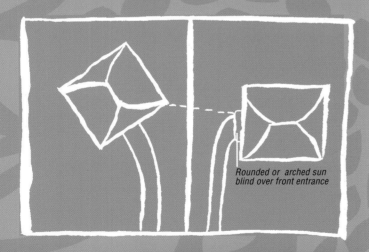

Rounded or arched sun blind over front entrance

- If the next door neighbor's roof has a poison arrow pointing into your front door, try the following. Put a round or arched sun blind or canopy at the front entrance. This repels the energy back. If you have ever walked into a restaurant that has an arched canopy over its entrance, then it's the same thing.

REMEDY
Front door cures.

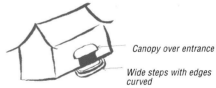

Canopy over entrance

Wide steps with edges curved

- Create wide, curved steps that get bigger at the bottom and slightly smaller at the top at the front door if possible. Even if there is room for only one or two steps, make them wide with curved edges. Wide steps with curved edges repel chi in the same manner as the canopy.

Convex mirror

- Put a convex mirror under the eves of your house, reflecting back at the poison arrow. Convex mirrors are raised round shaped mirrors on a flat base, and are available at most garages.

155

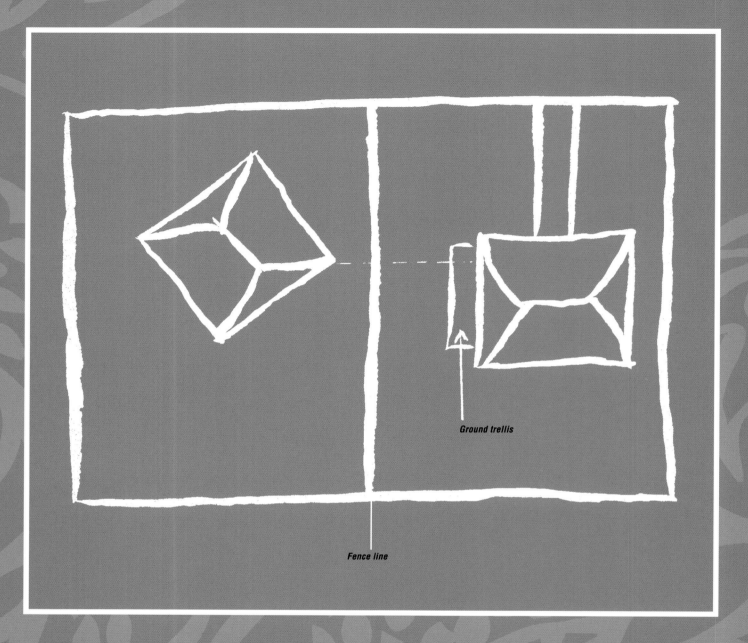

Ground trellis

Fence line

Bedroom cures

- Put a trellis along the fence line so it blocks out the poison arrow.

- Plant fast growing, tall trees along your fence line.

- A convex mirror is good for this problem too.

- If you cannot put a trellis on the fence line then put a ground trellis in between the fence and your bedroom window. Plant vines and hang plant baskets on it.

The aim is to create a barrier between the poison arrow and your entrance or bedroom window.

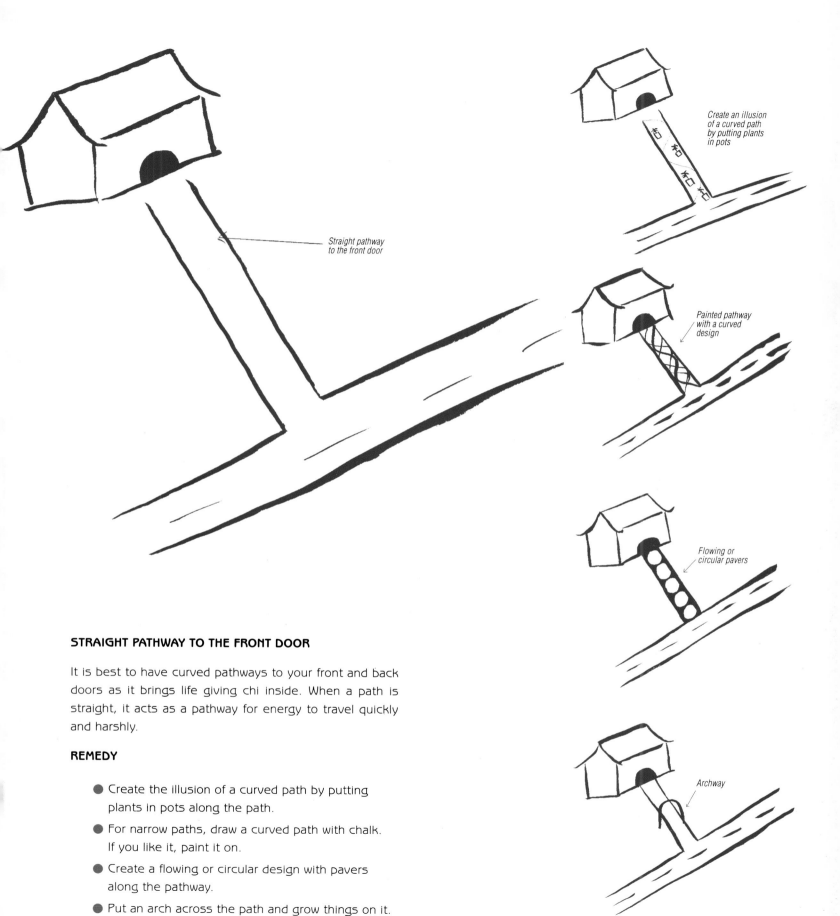

Create an illusion of a curved path by putting plants in pots

Straight pathway to the front door

Painted pathway with a curved design

Flowing or circular pavers

Archway

STRAIGHT PATHWAY TO THE FRONT DOOR

It is best to have curved pathways to your front and back doors as it brings life giving chi inside. When a path is straight, it acts as a pathway for energy to travel quickly and harshly.

REMEDY

- Create the illusion of a curved path by putting plants in pots along the path.
- For narrow paths, draw a curved path with chalk. If you like it, paint it on.
- Create a flowing or circular design with pavers along the pathway.
- Put an arch across the path and grow things on it.

High fence, trees
or shrubs

Clay objects
by front door

REMEDY

Plant trees, shrubs or install a high fence if you can. Do anything to obscure your vision from the power box. Power boxes are ugly and create unnecessary discomfort.

Due to the power box/pole representing the fire element, some Masters suggest putting an earth object like a stone, clay, or concrete fence between the house and pole. Other earth objects that can be used are terracotta, clay, stoneware, concrete, and/or ceramic products. These all help drain negative fire energy.

UGLY POWER POLE/BOX IN FRONT OF MY HOUSE

Not only do these obstacles look unsightly, they also lack a feng shui cure, apart of course, from using an earth cure barrier to symbolically drain the fire energy of the electricity. In the five element cycle, earth drains fire—it does not diffuse the electricity leaking. The amount of the leakage can be determined by a Trifield meter.

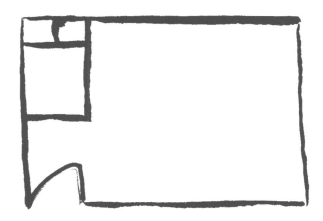

COFFIN POSITION

The coffin position is when the bed is directly aligned with the door, feet pointing towards the open doorway. Traditionally, undertakers took the coffin out feet first!

This is not a good way to sleep as it drains vital chi from the body. Many times my clients will complain of restless sleeps, feeling unwell, or inability to shake off bugs and viruses. Sometimes I find they sleep in the coffin position. As soon as the bed is removed from this position, a major difference is felt.

REMEDY

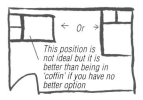

← Or →

This position is not ideal but it is better than being in 'coffin' if you have no better option

Change the bed position. THIS IS CRUCIAL AND HAS BEEN FOUND TO BE THE BEST CURE.

Close the door at night.

Hang a round crystal ball in the doorway to help circulate good chi.

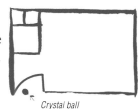

Crystal ball

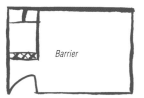

Barrier

Place a screen at the base of your bed in front of the door. Remove the screen during the day if it takes up space.

Place indoor plants between the base of your bed and doorway, and remember to close the door!!

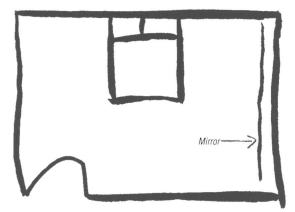

Mirror →

MIRRORED WARDROBE

According to certain Chinese feng shui theories, mirrors in the bedroom at night may deplete chi as you sleep, resulting in restless sleep, nightmares, insomnia, an active mind and inability to switch off at bedtime and/or unable to get out of bed each morning.

This is evident each time I find a client with mirrored wardrobes in their bedroom.

REMEDY

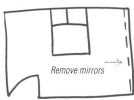

Remove mirrors →

Remove the mirrors from the wardrobe. So many clients comment on improved sleep and energy after doing this.

If you want to keep the mirrors, install a curtain rail across them. Simply close the curtains at night.

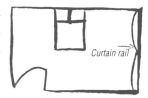

Curtain rail →

Screen

Place a Japanese screen or any other between the mirror and yourself to ensure that you cannot see yourself in the mirror. Fold and remove the screen during the day.

If you have a dresser with a mirror in the bedroom, make sure you cover it with a scarf, blanket or cloth at night while sleeping.

FRONT DOOR, BACK DOOR ALIGNMENT

You open the front door and see your back door or even a window.

Chi comes in and travels in a straight line out the back door again.

The effect of this could be money comes in and goes out again, or many bills but not enough money to go round, or there appears to be a drain on finances all the time.

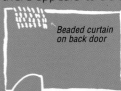

Beaded curtain on back door

REMEDY

Put a beaded curtain, curtains or a blind on the back door.

Table with flowers

If space prevails, place a round table between back and front door. Put a vase of flowers or healthy pot plant on the table.

Crystal ball

Hang a round crystal ball in the center of the house between back and front door alignment. The crystal helps disperse chi.

Screen or planter box

SLANTED CEILING

Having a slanted ceiling (not a slanted roof) may unbalance occupants after awhile. The subconscious will see an imbalance in shape, and this may create procrastination and/or confusion for occupants. The solution is to create a 'pretend' ceiling.

REMEDY

Put a wallpaper border at the lowest corner where it meets the slanted wall and continue across to the opposite wall. Do this on both ends. This creates a visual flat line border around the walls.

Alternatively hang pictures across the wall giving the impression of a flat ceiling.

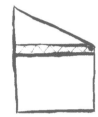

Place an uplight at either end of the lowest slant, shining up at the lowest part of the ceiling. Switch on for a few hours daily as this will push chi upwards.

The object of these remedies is to create a sense of a flat roof.

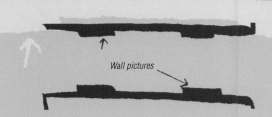

Wall pictures

Hang pictures on the walls so when people walk down they consciously or subconsciously take in the pictures. This helps distribute vital chi throughout the rooms.

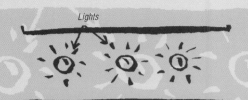

Lights

Install downlights along the corridor. This brings in light, light helps circulate chi.

Table and flowers

If the corridor is wide enough, place a long side table against the wall and put a lovely vase of flowers on it. This acts as a chi barrier.

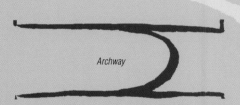

Archway

There are a few stores around which specialize in decorative finishes for houses. Put an arch or something similar centrally in the corridor. As chi travels it is slowed by the arch and then circulates at a more even pace.

Curtains

Alternatively, curtains are another interesting remedy to use.

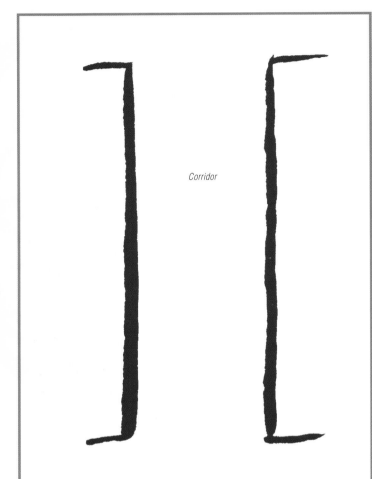

Corridor

LONG CORRIDORS

Corridors can be like sha chi as they funnel energy quickly. If there is a bedroom at the end, it may cause concern for the occupant.

DARK HOUSE

Houses are meant to be lived in and therefore lots of light, warmth and healthy activity is crucial to good feng shui. Houses with ivy growing around windows and doors, or lots of trees and bushes close to the house may hinder light and chi from entering. Balanced feng shui energy comes from allowing chi to enter via windows and doors that do not have obstructions.

REMEDY

If your house is dark, consider installing skylights. One thing to keep in mind when installing them is the house's natal chart or Flying Star chart (see p 171). A competent feng shui practitioner will be able to tell you the best place for a skylight.

Alternatively, switching internal lights on encourages good chi distribution. Oil burners and candles add a romantic feel as well as warmth and cosiness. It is best to burn uppernote oils such as bergamot, lemon and lemongrass to lift chi. Check with your aromatherapist to see which oils are considered uppernote oils.

Classical music, particularly Mozart is an excellent remedy to lift and lighten dark chi areas.

A great cure for a dark corridor is a picture of a rising sun with a picture light underneath it placed in a prominent area of the corridor. The rising sun symbolically lifts the chi and helps distribute it.

DRIPPING TAPS

Dripping taps represent a leakage of chi. No matter where the dripping tap is in the house it will drain the energy associated with this sector.

REMEDY

Fix it!

The house we live in should feel good for us to spend time in. Clutter, unwanted furniture and ugly objects only stagnate chi and may hinder opportunities coming our way. Create a house of beauty with objects and furnishings that suit your taste and help you feel at home in your surroundings.

Chapter 6

Easy to Understand "8 House Feng Shui"

*T*his is a compass based approach which uses the directions of north, south, east, southeast, west, northeast, northwest, and southwest to divide a house into eight sectors or palaces. The house is divided according to the eight directions taken from the center of it.

Some practitioners may prefer to use '8 House Feng Shui'; others may prefer to use Flying Star feng shui. Personally, I much prefer using Flying Star feng shui as I feel it is more precise and the results far reaching. Unfortunately, it does require study and takes time to understand. On the other hand, 8 House feng shui is far easier for the beginner to learn.

Not everyone wants to be a feng shui consultant so 8 House school may suit those who wish to study feng shui on a lighter note. Also it is a useful tool when determining a good area to work in and a good direction to face.

In 8 House feng shui the sitting or back of a building determines whether it belongs to the eastern or western group.

There are two types of houses—eastern and western life group houses. An eastern life house has its affinities with the north, south, southeast, and east directions. A western life house is aligned to west, northeast, northwest, and southwest directions. This rationale also applies to people.

The eight directions are present within each house, and it is important to understand which sector suits you best. To start, every house has a front and a back and we need to establish where they are.

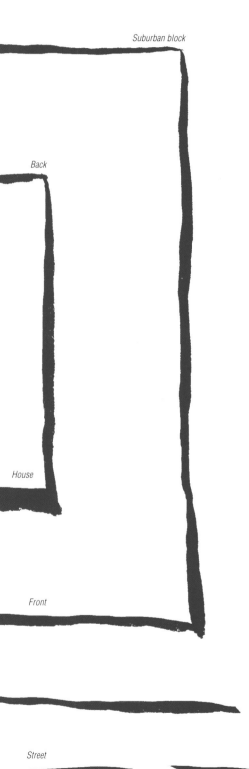

Suburban block

Back

House

Front

Street

Let's take a normal suburban block with a house. In this instance, the front of the house is the part that faces the street and the backyard is at the rear.

Private dwellings use the sitting direction (back of the building), while commercial premises use the facing (front of the building), to determine which group they belong to.

Say the house you occupy faces south, therefore the back or sitting faces north. As such, your house sits to the north and is considered an eastern life group house. Remember north, south, east, and southeast belong to the eastern life group.

Another example is your house faces east and the back sits to the west. Your house is considered a western life group house because west, northwest, southwest, and northeast belong to the western life group sectors or palaces.

If your house faces west and sits to the east it will belong to the eastern life group houses. If your house faces northwest and sits to the southeast, then it's an eastern life house.

People have personal ming kwa numbers and slot into eastern and western life groups too. Once you work out which group you belong to, you can work out whether your house suits you.

Following is a calculation to work out whether you are an eastern or western life person. Please keep in mind if you were born before February 4th; to use the year previous as your birth year. This is based on the Chinese new year dates.

CALCULATIONS

The calculations are as follows:
For males

Take the last two digits of your birth year, example 19 **62**.

Add the **6** and **2** which equals **8**. (6 + 2 = 8).

Deduct **8** from **10**.
(10 is the magic number used for this calculation).

The personal ming kwa number is **2**.

Another example is 19 **78**.

Add **7** and **8** which equals **15**. (7 + 8 = 15). Always add the two digits together until you get a single digit.

1 and **5** equals **6**. (1 + 5 = 6).

Deduct **6** from **10** (the magic number).

The personal ming kwa number is **4**.

If there is no remainder you are assigned the natal ming kwa number **9**.

If you are a **5** you take on the directions for the **2**. (see chart opposite).

The calculations for females are different:

Again take the year your were born using only the last two digits.

Example: 19 **55**.

Add **5** (5 is the magic number) to **55** which equals **60**. (5 + 55 = 60).

Divide **60** by **9** (9 is a magic number). It's the remainder we want and that is **6**. (60 divided by 9 = 54, with **6** remaining).

Another example is 19 **77**.

Add **5** to **77** which equals **82**. (5 + 77 = 82).

Divide **82** by **9** (82 divided by 9 = 9, with **1** remaining). The remainder is a ming kwa number of **1**.

One last example is 19 **45**.

Add **5** to **45** which equals **50**. (5 + 45 = 50).

Divide **50** by **9** (50 divided by 9 = 45, with **5** remaining).

If there is no remainder you are automatically assigned the natal ming kwa number of **9**. Additionally, if your ming kwa number is **5**, then use the directions for **8**. (see chart opposite)

By this stage it may sound confusing, but read on and it will become clear how this all fits together. When we work out our personal ming kwa number we find that it is aligned to a particular direction that will fit into either an eastern or western life groups.

Remember in the earlier chapters we discussed the five elements and their associations? The numbers from 1–9 are aligned with each direction, which in turn is associated with the five elements and certain colors as discussed in chapter 3 on the color ring. Your personal ming kwa number has four good directions that enhance your energy.

The ming kwa numbers and the associated directions are:

1 is associated with the direction north.

2 is associated with the direction southwest.

3 is associated with the direction east.

4 is associated with the direction southeast.

5 has no direction of its own but males take 2 and females take 8.

6 is associated with the direction northwest.

7 is associated with the direction west.

8 is associated with the direction northeast.

9 is associated with the direction south.

The above numbers then divide into eastern and western life groups.

EASTERN LIFE GROUP NUMBERS ARE: **1**, **3**, **4**, and **9**.

WESTERN LIFE GROUP NUMBERS ARE: **2**, **5**, **6**, **7**, and **8**.

If your ming kwa number is 1 then you are an eastern life group person and are bested suited to an eastern group house. Or if you are a 5, then you belong to the western life group but take on the directions of 2 if you are a male and 8 if you are female.

Say you are an eastern life group person living in an eastern group house. We know the directions of north, east, south, and southeast are good for you. However west, northwest, southwest, and northeast are not so good. We can make sure you position your bedroom, office, or any other favorite room in one of your favorable sectors or palaces of the house.

For example, your office might be located in the south palace which is good, but areas such as a toilet, bathroom, and laundry are suited for your unfavorable directions such as west, northwest, northeast and southwest. In other words it is better to put store rooms, laundry, toilet, bathroom, etc. in your unfavorable palaces. The bedroom, study, lounge room, and office should be put in your favorable palaces.

Please note that most Flying Star practitioners will position you according to the stars regardless of which direction the palace is in.

Each ming kwa number has four 'good' directions to face. The first best direction is prosperity; the second is health and healing; the third is harmony and to stop arguments; and the fourth is general success.

EASTERN LIFE GROUP

Kwa No	Prosperity	Health & Healing	Harmony/ Stop Arguments	General Success
1	Southeast	East	South	North
3	South	North	Southeast	East
4	North	South	East	Southeast
9	East	Southeast	North	South

WESTERN LIFE GROUP

Kwa No	Prosperity	Health & Healing	Harmony/ Stop Arguments	General Success
2	Northeast	West	Northwest	Southwest
6	West	Northeast	Southwest	Northwest
7	Northwest	Southwest	Northeast	West
8	Southwest	Northwest	West	Northeast

Say your ming kwa number is 5 and you are a male. You take the directions for 2. (Remember 5 people take on the number direction of 2 if male and 8 if female.) Say you want to work on creating prosperity in your life. Position your desk to face the northeast as this is your prosperity direction, or change your bed around so that when you are sleeping, your head points to northeast. When talking on the telephone to a client, make sure you face northeast. In other words you position yourself, your desk, chairs, and bed to face northeast, or any other of your favorable directions.

WHAT IF YOU ARE A WESTERN LIFE PERSON LIVING IN AN EASTERN LIFE HOUSE?

Okay, say you are a western life person and you are living in an eastern life house. Make sure you use rooms that are in the west, northwest, northeast and southwest part of your house. This is not always possible, so if you have a study in an unfavorable area such as southeast, make sure you position your furniture within your study to face either west, northwest, northeast or southwest.

This is called the art of placement.

The above explanation gives you a brief overall impression of 8 House feng shui which helps you position your furniture and room space according to your life group.

Of course, 8 House feng shui is more involved and is best studied with a Master. Remedies using the five elements are put into each palace or sector, to either drain or enhance the palace, understanding the dynamics of the five elements and how they relate to each palace.

Flying Star Feng Shui in Brief

*O*ver the years I have been taught Flying Star feng shui from various Masters. It appears to be a precise method for enabling change to take place in a person's life.

Flying Star does require studying with a competent Master for there are in-depth aspects to this fascinating science or art as some may call it, that need understanding.

A mathematical calculation is applied to the precise direction a house faces, and the time it has been built. This calculation is then superimposed over the house plan and divided into the eight compass directions of north, south, etc.

The numbers from 1–9 are used as each number represents a unique energy imprint. It is understanding how this energy impacts on the occupants that is the key to enhancing a person's life. Keeping in mind when remedies are put into place, they are always from the five element group such as fire, earth, metal, water, and wood.

The entire concept of feng shui is balance and understanding how to harmonize, enhance or drain the basic energy pattern surrounding you made up of the amazing ingredients of the five elements. This is the key to good feng shui.

Master Joseph Yu is a Master I have studied 'Flying Star' with. His explanations and interpretation of this extraordinary science is truly amazing. Flying Star Feng Shui impacts on our energy in both positive and life altering ways.

Chapter 7

Putting it all Together

木 土 水 火 金

All you need is a compass and your house plan.

STEP 1.
Throw away useless junk and get rid of clutter. Don't keep anything in case you may need it one day—if you don't use it now then get rid of it.

STEP 2.
Define your eight compass directions over your house plan and extend it out to your garden. Draw this up as an eight section pie chart over your house. Don't worry if it's not exact, make it approximate.

Write the direction in each sector.

STEP 3.
Work out whether you are an eastern or western life group person.

STEP 4.
Work out whether the house is an eastern or western life group house. Remember it's the sitting or physical back of your house that reveals whether it's an eastern or western group.

STEP 5.
Divide the house into your four favorable and not so favorable sectors or palaces.

STEP 6.
If possible arrange your lounge room, bedroom, study, and so forth in your good areas. However, this is not always possible. If a main room is in your unfavorable sector, then position your furniture to face one of your good directions.

For example, if you are a western life person and your study is in the eastern life area of the house such as north, southeast, east, or south, position your desk to face either west, northwest, southwest, or northeast. Although you study or work from an unfavorable area of the house, you still benefit by facing one of your good directions.

STEP 7.
Establish your color ring around your garden. This will take time so there is no need to hurry. Make it fun and do be inventive. Shapes and objects representing each element can be incorporated into each direction too.

STEP 8.
Be house proud and create an attractive entrance into your property. Invite healthy and prosperous chi into your house—make it look beautiful so you feel good when you enter.

Feng shui is a dynamic energy system that takes many years to study and understand its doctrine. Feng shui will enhance your life and help lead you to a healthier and more prosperous life.

However don't expect to sit back and let feng shui create a lifestyle for you while you do nothing to improve yourself emotionally, mentally, physically, and spiritually. According to feng shui doctrine there are three types of luck:

- Heaven luck, - that which we are born with.
- Man luck, - the house we live in.
- Earth luck, - the land the house is built upon and its surrounding landscape.

If we have poor earth and man luck but good heaven luck, our integrity of being will help our environment to a large degree. If we move to a house that has good earth and man luck, then our life will be enriched greatly.

However, if we are born with poor heaven luck, and live in poor man and earth luck, then we may experience many obstacles in our life. This may continue until one becomes aware of subconscious patterns, outdated thoughts and lack of integrity towards others.

My Qi Gong Masters have taught me that you can never change your heaven luck but you can certainly improve the quality of your heaven luck—in other words—improve your integrity of being. This is done by practising yoga, Qi Gong, Tai Chi, Meditation, Martial Arts, integrity of speech, thought and action. In other words living the life of an integral being.

There is an old story and it goes like this.

A young thief approaches a great yoga and feng shui Master and asks him to teach him how to walk through walls.

The Master asks the thief why. To this the thief replies, "I wish to walk through walls so I can steal people's belongings and live a rich life."

The Master contemplates on this for a while and finally replies, " I will teach you how to walk through walls so you may steal people's belongings, but it is on one condition."

The thief asks what the condition is and the Master replies, "You must come and live with me and follow my lifestyle and practice it as your own. In the end you will be able to walk through walls." The thief agrees to this.

Many years pass and the thief lives the same lifestyle as the Master does; eventually learning the secret of walking through walls. However, he no longer wishes to steal people's belongings because he has reached 'Enlightenment' and lives a rich and wondrous life, for he has become the Master himself, full of integrity, love, honesty and right action—he is an empowered being.

Feng shui can help you to become an empowered being.

Dare to use the power of feng shui!

May you all be blessed with good feng shui and prosperity always.

Terri Rew

Photography Credits

Country House
Cox Architects
Photography: Tim Griffith pp12, 13 (left, below); p14 (above)

Kensington Restoration
Cox Architects
Photography: Max Dupain p13 (above)

Villa Saga
Helin & Siitonen Architects
Photography: Rauno Träskalin pp14, 15 (right, opposite); p148 (right)

Kumu Honua
Media Five Ltd
Photography: Tim Griffith p16 (below)

Giovando Residence
Jeff Harnar Architects
Photography: Douglas Kahn/Jeff Harnar Architects p16 (right)

Jarvis Residence
House + House
Photography: Steven House p17

Residence in Chestnut Hill
Susan Maxman & Partners
Photography: Tom Bernard p18

Goderich Street Housing
Cox Architects
Photography: Patrick Bingham-Hall p19

Moverly Green Housing
Cox Architects
Photography: Patrick Bingham-Hall pp20, 21

The Cornerstone
Cox Architects
Photography: Patrick Bingham-Hall pp22, 23

Ocean House
Cox Architects
Photography: Patrick Bingham-Hall pp27, 42, 43

Ocean Front Retreat
Ivan Bereznicki Associates, Inc.
Photography: Steve Rosenthal pp28–31, 144

The Homestead
House + House
Photography: courtesy *Fine Homebuilding*/Chuck Miller p32

Forest View Residence
House + House
Photography: Christoper Irion p33

Private Residence
House + House
Photography: Gerald Ratto p34

Stine Residence
House + House
Photography: courtesy *House Beautiful*/Christopher Irion p35

Plinth House III
Kanner Architects
Photography: Mark Lohman p36

Noronha's house
Tomás Taveira
Photography: courtesy Tomás Taveira p37

Grandview Estate
House + House
Photography: Steven House pp38, 39, 44, 45

Langmaid Residence
House + House
Photography: David Livingston p40

Dan House
Malibu, California, USA
Photography: Erhard Pfeiffer p41

Arrabal
Antonio H Ravazzani & Associates
Photography: Antonio Ravazzani pp49, 68

Private House
Du Bose Associates, Inc Architects with Theurkauf & Company
Photography: Robert Benson Photography pp56, 57

Highland House
Hardy Holzman Pfeiffer Associates
Photography: Tom Kessler pp58, 59

Rotunda House
Architects 49 Limited
Photography: Skyline Studio p60

Leader House
Alfredo De Vido Architects
Photography: courtesy Alfredo De Vido Architects pp61–65

The Warehouse
Michael Graves Architect
Photography: courtesy Michael Graves Architect/Marek Bulaj pp66, 67, 84 (above)

Residence in Chestnut Hill
Susan Maxman & Partners
Photography: Tom Bernard p69

David Alan House
Alfredo De Vido Architects
Photography: Norman McGrath p70

1 White Pine Road
Alfredo De Vido Architects
Photography: courtesy Alfredo De Vido Architects p71 (above)

Casa di Fontanellato
Architetto Aurelio Cortesi
Photography: courtesy Architetto Aurelio Cortesi p71 (left)

Glanz Residence
House + House
Photography: Claudio Santini p73 (opposite)

Harstene House
Anderson Anderson Architecture
Photography: Michael Scarbrough p72 (top & bottom)

Private Residence
Looney Ricks Kiss Architects
Photography: Jeffrey Jacobs/Architectural Photography pp74, 75

Apartment 61 East, 86 Street
Alfredo De Vido Architects
Photography: Norman McGrath p76 (above)

Gary Residence
House + House Architects
Photography: Claudio Santini p76 (center), p77

A House for Two Architects
House + House Architects
Photography: Steven House pp78, 79, 88, 89

Baan Premika
Architects 49 Limited
Photography: Shussana Satanavapark p80 (above)

Minton House
Alfredo De Vido Architects
Photography: courtesy Alfredo De Vido Architects p80 (below); Fred Charles p113 (above)

Oliver Residence
Inglese Architecture
Photography: Alan Geller p81

Kessler house
Alfredo De Vido Architects
Photography: courtesy Alfredo De Vido Architects pp82, 83

Architects House and Office
Alfredo De Vido Architects
Photography: courtesy Alfredo De Vido Architects p84 (top left)

Courtyard House
Anderson Anderson Architecture
Photography: Roger Turk p84 (bottom left)

Private Residence
Looney Ricks Kiss Architects, Inc.
Photography: Scott McDonald/Hedrich-Blessing p85

Chason Residence Addition & Remodel
House + House
Photography: Alan Geller p86

Urban Condominium
Looney Ricks Kiss Architects, Inc.
Photography: Scott McDonald/Hedrich-Blessing p87

The Tallai House
Philip Follent Architects
Photography: Luke Rowlinson p89 (left)

Hismen Hin-nu Terrace
Pyatok Associates
Photography: Michael Pyatok p90 (top left); Janet Delaney p90 (top right)

Pennock Farmstead Restoration
Susan Maxman & Partners
Photography: Catherine Bogert p91

Corman Guest House
Regina Pizzinini & Leon Luxemburg
Photography: Dominique Vorillon pp92, 93

Villa Petite
Regina Pizzinini & Leon Luxemburg
Photography: Gert von Bassewitz pp94, 95

House, Schoenfels
Regina Pizzinini & Leon Luxemburg
Photography: Yvan Klein pp96–99

House, Niederthai
Regina Pizzinini & Leon Luxemburg
Photography: Gert von Bassewitz pp100–105

Röckenwagner House
Regina Pizzinini & Leon Luxemburg
Photography: Erhard Pfeiffer p106 (top), p107; Jeremy Samuleson p106 (bottom)

Trah House
Regina Pizzinini & Leon Luxemburg
Photography: Jörg Hemple Photodesign pp108–111

Doyle Residence
Jeff Harnar Architects
Photography: Douglas Kahn p112

Villa Mira
Helin & Siitonen Architects
Photography: Titta Lumio p113 (left, below left & right)

Wertheimer House
Alfredo De Vido Architects
Photography: Robert Lautman p114

Farese House
Alfredo De Vido Architects
Photography: Paul Warchol p115

De Vido house
Alfredo De Vido Architects
Photography: House Beautiful p116 (above & left); Hans Namuth p116 (right); Norman McGrath p117

222 Columbia Heights
Alfredo De Vido Architects
Photography: *New York Times* pp118, 119

McConomy Poolhouse, Garden & Pavilions
Alfredo De Vido Architects
Photography: courtesy Alfredo De Vido Architects p120; Norman McGrath p121

Drake House
Alfredo De Vido Architects
Photography: courtesy Alfredo De Vido Architects pp122–125; Paul Warchol pp126, 127

New Technologies Building, Curtin University of Technology
Cox Architects
Photography: Patrick Bingham-Hall pp128, 129

Broome Street Housing
Cox Architects
Photography: Patrick Bingham-Hall pp130, 131

Private Residence
Looney Ricks Kiss Architects, Inc.
Photography: Jeffrey Jacobs/Architectural Photography p132 (above & center)

Palmer Residence
Looney Ricks Kiss Architects, Inc.
Photography: Jeffrey Jacobs/Mims Studios p132 (right)

Crooked Pightle House
Robert Adam Architects
Photography: Joe Low p133

Anawalt House
Moore Ruble Yudell
Photography: Timothy Hursley p134 (top)

Mr Eaton's Residence
Architects 49 Limited
Photography: Somkid Piampiyachart/Skyline p134 (bottom)

Stewart House
Helliwell + Smith•Blue Sky Architecture
Photography: John Fulker p135

Langmaid Residence
House + House
Photography: Mark Darley/Esto pp136, 137

Alta residence
House + House
Photography: Mark Johnson pp138, 140

Greenwich House
Cox Architects
Photography: David Moore p139 (top right)

Donner House Extension
Juhani Katainen Architects
Photography: Hannu Koivisto p139 (bottom right)

Ka Hale Kukuna Residence
House + House
Photography: Michael French p141

Governor's Residence
Du Bose Associates, Inc. Architects
Photography: Robert Benson pp142, 143

Gersch Residence
House + House
Photography: Gerald Ratto p145; Philip Harvey p147

Duplex Development at Fraser Road
Bolig Design Group Limited
Photography: Richard Woldendorp p146

Inman House
Moore Ruble Yudell
Photography: Timothy Hursley p148 (above)